A Practical Guide to Simple Happiness

Larry Gross
Illustrated by Mark Lieberman

A Practical Guide to Simple Happiness

ISBN-13: 978-0692-7998-64
ISBN-10: 0692-799-869

For more information, or to communicate with
author Larry Gross, visit:
www.apracticalguidetosimplehappiness.com

Or, email:
Lgross7798@yahoo.com

Disclaimer

This book details the author's personal experiences with and opinions about relaxation and happiness. The author is not a licensed therapist.

The author and publisher are providing this book and its contents on an "as is" basis and make no representations or warranties of any kind with respect to this book or its contents. The author and publisher disclaim all such representations and warranties, including, for example, warranties of merchantability and advice for a particular purpose. In addition, the author and publisher do not represent or warrant that the information accessible via this book is accurate, complete or current.

The statements made about products and services have not been evaluated by the U.S. government. Please consult with your own legal or accounting professional regarding the suggestions and recommendations made in this book.

Except as specifically stated in this book, neither the author or publisher, nor any authors, contributors or any other representatives, will be liable for damages arising out of or in connection with the use of this book. This is a comprehensive limitation of liability that applies to all damages of any kind, including (without limitation) compensatory; direct, indirect or consequential damages; loss of data, income or profit; loss of or damage to property; and claims of third parties.

You understand that this book is not intended as a substitute for consultation with a licensed medical, legal or accounting professional. Before you begin any change to your lifestyle in any way, you will consult a licensed professional to ensure that you are doing what's best for your situation.

This book provides content related to relaxation topics. As such, use of this book implies your acceptance of this disclaimer.

Table of Contents

Introduction

This is a book about change. How I have changed from an unhappy person to a much happier person. The content of this book is what I am currently doing, and have done in my life to be happier.

Am I happy all of the time? No. I'm not sure it is possible to be happy all the time, but the jury is still out! When you're ill, are you happy? Or if you hurt yourself and are in pain, are you happy in that moment, most likely not. However, I have reached a consistent level of happiness that I feel is worth sharing, so I wrote this book.

I want the book to stimulate YOU to venture out from your normal routine and try something different—or maybe just to think about something you have never considered before—to bring more happiness into your life. Maybe there is a different way, a better way for you to allow happiness into your life. All I know how to present is what makes me happy. I can't and won't tell you what makes YOU happy because only YOU truly know what that is. There will be times in this book that I ask theoretical questions... because I have no idea myself what the answers are. The idea is for you to think, contemplate, and make positive changes in your life.

My search for happiness has been a lifelong adventure. I learned from an early age that having money didn't necessarily mean you would be happy.

I was raised in a family that had money. From what my parents told me, we seemed to have more money than most of my friends. I noticed however, my parents were not very happy people. And that, of course, affected their children. In fact, my friends with less money seemed happier than my family and me. My mom drank a lot, and my dad was bitter about this, in addition to business disappointments.

So, having an understanding that money doesn't buy happiness put me on the road (which I am still on) to find out what does. Instead of trying to make lots of money (my parents' goal for me), my goal was always to be happy. In fact—like I said previously—if it's possible, I want to find out how to be happy all of the time! WITHOUT THE USE OF DRUGS AND ALCOHOL!

Throughout my life there were two major influences that lead me toward writing this book. One was the constant bombardment of negativity I received during the majority of my life, compliments of the media, watching the daily and nightly news on TV, or listening to it on the radio. On top of that, as the years go by, movies and television shows are getting much more violent and graphic than they used to be. Even cartoons and especially video games are loaded with death and killing. I know every one of you can relate to what I am talking about! We live in the same world...

The other long-term influence that caused me to write this book was what I had mentioned earlier about my childhood and upbringing.

Well, one day I had had enough! I can't pinpoint a particular moment, or tragic event, or news story that put me over the edge, but I fell...

...the result being, I had to do something! So, instead of complaining about the sorrows of the world (which I would do at great lengths to my friends), and with me being on my own personal quest to find happiness, I made the decision to help.

My goal in writing this book is to share with you some of my beliefs; changes in behaviors, attitudes, and routines I have made in my life that help me (and I hope will help you) create more peace, contentment, and happiness in everyday living- thus creating a happier world!

Chapter 1

If It Isn't Fun, Don't Do It!

The first guideline is pretty self-explanatory, isn't it? If you don't like doing something, well... just don't do it. Wouldn't it be great if it were just that simple? Unfortunately, there are lots of tasks in life- mundane and otherwise- that have to be completed, whether we enjoy doing them or not. For example: doing the dishes.

I can't explain my aversion to doing the dishes, but it's there! I know people who don't mind doing the dishes, and believe it or not, I even know people who enjoy the task! So why is it possible for some people to enjoy a chore that other people hate? I believe it's because we all have our own way of viewing the world. We are each individuals with our own unique perspective and perceptions. So where do we go from here?

Since we each have our unique way of experiencing the world, we as individuals have to figure out ways to make the mundane tasks in our lives as enjoyable as possible, or at the very least, tolerable. Remember: we control our own happiness by the way we view life. We determine what is enjoyable to us.

I believe we first need to figure out what we don't like about the particular task at hand. As I said earlier, I hated to do the dishes. Looking at a pile of dishes was overwhelming to me. Where do I start? Which dish do I wash first? How can I possibly clean any dish when the sink I am supposed to wash AND rinse in is PILED up with dishes? I'm getting a little worked up just thinking about it!

My solution was to get a separate tub to put the dirty dishes in to soak. That way the sink was clear to wash AND rinse the dishes.

I also listen to music and away I go! This is my way of making an un-enjoyable task more enjoyable. In addition, I have adopted a mindset that I call the "one less" principle...

Chapter 2

The One Less Principle

When I was about ten or eleven years old, I was faced with the annual task of raking the yard every fall. There were thousands and thousands of leaves that had to be raked. If I kept looking at the yard while I was raking, I got overwhelmed and, quite frankly, angry at having to do the task. I'm not sure if I was hit on the head with a branch or what, but one day I had the realization that there were a limited number of leaves to rake up, not an infinite number. They weren't going to fall forever. At some point during my raking I found myself thinking "one less." One less leaf; one less stroke; one less pile; one less dish... Get the idea? It comforted me to know I was making progress on the task at hand.

Another illustration of this principle came about when I was helping a friend prepare a room to be painted. This particular room was about twelve feet by twelve feet, and used by a drummer as a practice room. Instead of installing acoustic tile for soundproofing, the drummer stapled sound proofing material on all four walls... and the ceiling. After removing the sound proofing material, the room was covered with literally THOUSANDS of staples! The only way to remove them was one at a time, with a pair of needle nose pliers. Another friend who was helping me with the task was getting all worked up and started complaining.

"How could somebody do something like this?"

"What were they thinking?"

On and on he went! I just started pulling staples, and with each one that I pulled, I thought "one less." I told my friend about the "one less" principle, but he quit working shortly after in total frustration. I completed the task in about 7 hours.

I believe most tasks in life are a lot simpler and enjoyable when one has developed a system that is suited for him or her to get the task completed. My system might not work for you. *You* are going to have to come up with your own unique way to complete a task if you want to maximize your enjoyment. Nobody can develop a better system that will work for you, than *you!*

Another important point is you accept the task for what it is... not how it got that way, or why it got that way. These issues if need be, can be addressed at another time. The task needs to be completed, so complete it! Again, we control our happiness though our own perceptions and attitudes.

Chapter 3

Treat Yourself Like Royalty!

What do you think of when you hear the word "royalty," or "The Royal Family?" Do you think of a life of leisure, comfort, luxury, and pampering? I do! What is the difference between those people and you? Well, those people happened to be born into a situation of leisure. What about the rest of us? Don't we deserve to live a life of comfort and to be pampered? I think we do! The difference between royalty and us is we have to pamper ourselves.

I believe it's very important to attempt to feel like royalty as much as possible. This does not mean to take on an elitist attitude, or to think you are better than anybody else. All this means is you start treating yourself better by honoring yourself. What do I mean by "honor?" The definition I think fits best concerning this guide is: "to show high regard or appreciation." The key is: you are going to do this to yourself.

Someone told me I should treat myself the way I treat my best friend whom I greatly respect. I am attempting to do this. In the past, when I made a mistake, I would call myself all sorts of derogatory names like "dumb-ass," "idiot," and oh, my favorite..."moron." I have never, nor would I ever call my best friend or anybody else these names, and I have rarely felt anger toward them for making an honest mistake. I, as I stated above, am another story.

What is a mistake, anyway? Isn't it an unintended result or consequence? Does anybody try to make a mistake? I think not! So why can't we be as kind to ourselves as we are to our best friend? Maybe NOW is the time we start treating ourselves like the Kings and Queens we truly are, and bring more happiness into our lives.

The Golden Rule states that you should do unto others as you would have them do unto you, right? Well, I am going to add a little to that...do unto others AND YOURSELF, as you would have them do unto you. In other words, treat others as you wish to be treated, and treat yourself the same way.

In addition to mentally treating yourself like royalty, I believe you can foster more happiness by how and what you decide to purchase...

Chapter 4

Purchasing to Foster Happiness

We live in a society that rewards and praises "getting a great deal" on our purchases. If you bought something for the lowest price, then you're a winner, right? I have a slightly different way at looking at this.

First of all, only buy items you need. Some people will buy items just because they "got a great deal," regardless of whether they need them or not. Is it a great deal if you never use it? What if it doesn't fit exactly right and you're uncomfortable wearing it?

My second suggestion is that you only buy quality items. You are worth it! Besides, in the long run, it usually pays off. Many people are willing to sacrifice comfort and happiness for the sake of getting a good deal.

I believe price should be a secondary consideration. The first step of course, is to decide what you want to purchase. Then, I recommend you look for the highest quality version of that particular item and learn what makes it high quality. You don't want to buy junk! Once you have completed your research, you're ready to shop around for the best deal. You have worked hard for your money; don't waste it buying crap!

Another consideration I think about is how often I will use this particular item? Am I going to use it every day, once a week, once a month...once a year? If I use it every day, then how many hours per day?

Recently I purchased a new car—new for me and used for somebody else. As I started shopping around, I'd look on Craig's List, EBay, or just stop in at various car lots. What I realized was that I had too many cars to choose from, and couldn't make up my mind. I knew what I wanted the car to have, and how much money I wanted to spend. Knowing these things was a big help! To narrow down the search, I decided to buy a car from a friend of mine who owned a car lot. I then looked up his lot on-line and watched his inventory for 3 months. Finally he had 3 cars that fit my criteria. I researched all 3 cars. Interestingly enough, the research showed that even though the 2 cars I *didn't* buy were less expensive AND had fewer miles on them, the car I did get was the better buy in the long run... due to its gas mileage, quality, and dependability.

Not only will quality items save you money in the long term, they will aid you with better performance, resulting in less stress and less work. I am going to give examples of how we can honor ourselves through the use of our household items...

Chapter 5

Honoring Ourselves With Our Household Items

The first item we're going to look at is the bed we sleep on. Is it comfortable? When you "hit the sack," are you happy to be in YOUR bed? Do you get a good night's sleep?

When I was growing up—being the youngest in the family—I got all of the "hand-me-down" beds. Yes, I was fortunate to have a bed to sleep on—however, it wasn't very comfortable and was wearing out. For years, I played "avoid the spring" that was sticking me in the back when I tried to sleep. I can't remember how long it took for me to save up for a new mattress, but finally I bought one. Boy was it worth it! No spring to avoid and a good night's sleep!

You see, I figured I spend an average of 8 hours every night of my life in bed, so it would be worth the extra money to buy a quality mattress. I did shop around and also got a good deal.

Along the same lines as the bed, I was given some hand-me-down sheets and pillowcases. They were OK, not nearly an issue like the mattress, but Mom insisted on getting linens made out of 50% polyester and 50% cotton. She did this so they wouldn't get wrinkled in the dryer. She chose appearance over comfort. In the case of a good night sleep, I choose *comfort*.

I would occasionally get to sleep over at my grandma's house. She had the softest, most comfortable, 100% cotton sheets. She unfortunately passed away when I was twelve years old, but the memory of those sheets stuck with me. When I got older, you guessed it- I bought my own 100% cotton sheets.

I learned a few things along the way about sheets. They are not all created equal. You will want to get the highest thread count possible. Mine are 600-thread count. I think you can get a thread count as high as 1200. As soon as mine wear out, I'm upgrading! Let me tell you though, the 600's are luxurious. Even the 400's are mighty comfortable! 100% cotton sheets are not cheap, however. They may cost around $80 to $120 for a Queen-sized set.

Again, I shopped around and happened to find a store that was going out of business, and I paid much less.

Even if you pay retail for your sheets, it's clearly worth the extra money and it's one way to treat yourself like royalty. They might be a little more expensive, but they should last you roughly five to ten years. And as a bonus, the more you wash them, the softer they get. Let me tell you; when I crawl into bed, I am *so* comfortable. Just like a king should be!

Make the entire sleep experience as comfortable as possible. Shop around for the perfect pillow for you. Mine happens to be a feather pillow, but that might not be the best choice for you. While you are out shopping, make it a fun experience. Remember, you are shopping for the Royal Family: YOU!

To sum it up, a person spends an average of 8 hours per day in bed. Can you think of any reason why you wouldn't want to spend it in maximum comfort?

The next item I would like to bring up for consideration is the showerhead in your bathroom. How many of you have that cheap three-to-five dollar model that has no adjustments, no pulsating actions, and—truth be told—doesn't give you a very enjoyable shower? I figure that most people spend ten to twenty minutes per day in the shower. I'm a person who loves and needs a morning shower to get the day off to a good start. I admit it! I had that three-dollar showerhead until I visited my sister and took a shower at her place. "Oh, my God," my life was transformed! Well… not literally, but I had a much more enjoyable shower due to that showerhead.

Her particular showerhead cost around forty dollars, but was much more powerful than mine, had two adjustments, *and* was a water saver to boot! So for an extra thirty-seven dollars, I take a much more enjoyable shower for fifteen minutes each day. I have had my showerhead for about five years now.

Of course, then you get out of the shower and dry off with a towel, wrap it around you, brush your teeth, comb your hair, and basically start getting ready to go out in the world. That's what I did until I discovered what I will call the "comfy robe."

Did you see the first *Beverly Hills Cop* movie, starring Eddie Murphy? At the end of the movie he purchases 2 Beverly Palm Hotel robes. They are lavish and comfortable. This is what I am talking about! After you dry off with your towel, you could reach for a luxurious all-cotton robe that you slip on. Instead of having cold shoulders and legs, you are now wrapped in a soft, comfy robe that is warm and dry. Along these same lines, wearing a comfortable pair of slippers would turn your morning ritual into a complete experience of comfort and leisure.

Let's say your morning ritual takes about fifteen minutes. I have shown you a way to be in comfort and luxury for eight and a half hours out of your twenty-four hour day. What about the remaining fifteen and a half hours?

How can we use our time more efficiently, thus creating more leisure, free time, and happiness? I believe one habit to develop is to make a daily "to-do" list.

Chapter 6

Developing a "To-Do" List

Developing a "to-do" list will allow you to organize your thoughts and thus organize your day. By organizing your day, I believe you will find that your level of stress will decrease, and your level of calmness and happiness will increase. This is because you are tackling your day with a plan of action... instead of haphazardly. In other words, your pre-planning will help eliminate mistakes that can cause you to lose precious time and money. The smoother your day flows, the happier you will be!

You can do this for your home or business. If it's for your home, take around 10-15 minutes of quiet time (before the kids get up, or after they leave) to brainstorm all of the things you want to accomplish during the day. Then, prioritize the list- most important tasks first, and so on. If errands need to be run, run the errands in a sequence that flows from one to another. Take your list with you. When you accomplish an item, scratch it off the list. I get so much satisfaction when I scratch something off the list. In a way, I am patting myself on the back for getting something done.

If you have a task such as cleaning out the refrigerator, don't start another task until you finish the first task you've begun. Nothing is worse (in my opinion) than being in the middle of several projects, and completing none of them.

I worked at a major hotel chain as Banquet manager. Generally, my work schedule was from 8:00 AM to 5:00 PM, Monday through Saturday. If I wanted to get to work by 8, I had to leave my house at 7, due to rush hour traffic. If I left work at 5 to head home, it was also an hour drive. What I learned to do was leave my house at 6:30, which got me to the hotel by 7. If I left the hotel at 6, I would arrive at home at 6:30.

Some of you might think I was wasting an hour of my day by leaving earlier in the morning and later in the evening. I didn't look at it that way! To me it was worth giving the extra time; not only did I avoid the stress caused by driving in rush-hour traffic, I saved an hour of travel time, and I saved money on gasoline. I'm sure some of you are wondering what any of this has to do with making a "to do list"?

With the extra time I created by arriving at work early and leaving work late, I had some quiet time to plan my workday. Like at home, when I arrived at work I made a "to do list" of everything I wanted to accomplish for the day, and then I prioritized my tasks. As I completed my tasks, I scratched them off the list. A day rarely went by that new items weren't added to the list. On most days some items didn't get completed. At the end of the day, I started a new "to-do" list and the uncompleted items were transferred to it. By making a new "to-do" list at the end of the day, I was able to leave all of my work "at the office."

This allowed me to not think about what I had to do at work when I was at home, and enabled me to spend a stress free, leisurely, fun evening at home, or if I wanted, I could do a little exercise...

Chapter 7

Diet and Exercise

One thing that makes happy me is when I am physically fit. I have always been athletic, primarily because I enjoyed playing sports and was pretty good at the various sports I participated in. As the years have gone by, the sports I can play have gotten fewer and fewer. Whereas I used to play baseball, soccer, basketball and tennis; now I am down to tennis. When I got into my upper thirties, I hurt my shoulder playing baseball and started pulling my hamstrings on a regular basis playing soccer. A hamstring takes about 6 weeks to heal and it got to the point where I felt it wasn't worth playing any more. Basketball was just becoming generally too painful to recover from so that left me with tennis. I added hiking, walking, and/ or joining a gym.

When I was younger my goal was to be a "stud." Now I just want to maintain an average weight for my height and be healthy. Over the past 3 years I had gained an extra 10 pounds. Now that might not sound like much, considering it took me 3 years to accumulate, but it was all in the form of belly fat and when I looked in the mirror I wasn't happy with myself.

For a long time I wasn't happy with myself, which meant every time I looked in the mirror at my bulging belly I criticized myself. I had a choice, I could continue to criticize myself, or do something about my fat belly and be happier with myself.

The thing was, I never stopped exercising, but I started eating lots of late night peanut butter and jelly sandwiches, Reese cups, Twix, lots of snack pints of coconut ice cream, potato chips, Cheetos... the list goes on! Did I mention I have a sweet tooth?

At that point in my life, my morning routine was much different than it is today—especially my diet. I was doing Qi Gong stretches, soaking my feet, and meditating. I was eating 3 pieces of regular pork bacon and 3 eggs. Sometimes I would make an egg sandwich with lots of butter! When I went out to eat, I would usually order pancakes with real maple syrup, bacon, eggs, toast and hash browns.

I had some financial troubles (which I will talk about later in the book) that caused me to share a house with 2 friends of mine. One of them was really into working out and that motivated me. I first added pushups to my morning routine, but admittedly I could only do 10. After a few weeks I was up to 15, and a few weeks later I was at 20. I stopped at 20 because my right shoulder would really hurt if I did more than 20. In addition to the pushups, I looked for ways to get exercise. I volunteered to cut the lawn, just for the chance to exercise. About 8 months later, I added sit-ups to the routine. Like the pushups, I started with a small amount and worked my way up.

With me doing all of this exercise, I knew I was getting in better shape, I had lost a few pounds, but the belly fat was hanging tough. The problem was I hadn't changed my diet and/or I wasn't getting enough exercise.

The first thing I did was to limit my breakfast to 2 eggs and 2 pieces of turkey bacon. I also started reading every label on food I would potentially buy. ANYTHING with HYDROGENATED whatever goes back on the shelf. I was fortunate to find all-natural 94% lean turkey bacon, so I switched to that.

I was still doing lots of snacking and so was my belly fat! I realized I needed some additional motivation, so I hired a very attractive health/life coach. I know myself well enough to realize she could motivate me. Now don't get me wrong, I was already motivated, I just needed an extra boost. She gives me lots of information on what foods to eat, what not to eat, great encouragement and a few healthy recipes.

Instead of going out to eat the majority of the time, I cook most of my food now. I cook using exclusively olive oil or coconut oil, making lots and lots of stir-fries. They are easy to make, healthy, fast and delicious!

I cut out bread, sugar, fruit, candy bars, potato chips and most carbohydrates. Let me tell you, it wasn't easy, especially when I first started! My craving for sugar was strong! Every time I went (and continue to go) through the line at the grocery store, all of the candy bars call my name… "Buy me, Larry… buy me, Larry!" It was all I could do to get out of there alive!! LOL! As time went on, I lost the sugar cravings, and so will you!

I also joined a gym. The gym only cost $10 per month. I walk 3 miles on the treadmill 3 to 4 times a week. When the weather gets nice, I will walk outside. To date I have lost 5 pounds and almost all of the belly fat. I have completed 3 months of my 6 month program and have no doubt I will reach my goal.

Why am I telling you this? One reason is to let you know you don't have to kill yourself to lose weight. Start slowly; if you only walk for 15 minutes per day to start, its OK... go at your own pace. If you can take a walk after you eat, do it! It gets you out of the house and is a good way to clear your head. In some respects this is like the "one less" principle (Chapter 2) in that slow and easy will win the race: each step you take on a walk, each pushup you do, every candy bar you do not eat, will- little by little- help you reach your goal. In addition to physically feeling better, I mentally feel better because I am actively making positive changes in my life.

The idea is for you to feel good about yourself! The better you feel about yourself, the happier you will be.

As long as we are talking about feeling good, one thing I highly recommend is soaking your feet!

Chapter 8

Slow Down and Soak Your Feet

Soaking your feet is one of the greatest gifts of comfort, pampering, and mental health I can think of. It's very simple and extremely inexpensive. All you have to do is get a plastic tub, fill it with hot water and stick your feet in it. Really, that's all there is to it! I add Epsom salt and some lavender oil, or anything I think smells good. I put a towel underneath the tub in case I spill any water. Then I put on some relaxing music and close my eyes. The water stays hot for around fifteen to twenty minutes. I focus on the music and how good my feet feel. And they feel really, really good! For that time period, I forget all of my troubles and slow down.

Recently, some friends visited me from Alaska (a couple and their 6 year old son). I did my daily routine of soaking my feet and urged them to give it a try. They loved it so much, now it is a part of their daily routine (including their son's). If you get nothing out of this book other than soaking your feet, it will be worth the read.

Truthfully, I've never met anyone who didn't enjoy soaking their feet! It's just a matter of actually doing it! Sometimes I soak my feet as part of my morning ritual, or sometimes I do it when I get home from work. See what works for you. I will usually take this time to meditate also…

Chapter 9

Meditation

Meditation—to me—is no more than relaxing the mind from thinking. Anything we create in our world, we have to think about first. This includes stress. The less you think, the less stress you have. Obviously you have to think most of the time to survive. I am suggesting for maybe fifteen minutes per day, you schedule some time to do your best to shut it all down.

There are various ways to meditate. One way is to focus on your breathing; in through your nose, filling your abdomen, and exhale comfortably. I will even say to myself…"in comes the love, out goes the fear". Focusing on your breathing keeps you from thinking about anything else. If you find you start thinking about other things besides your breathing, refocus.

A friend of mine was a busy executive during his working years. His job was very stressful and he started having some physical problems. He went to the doctor and was told he "had better learn to relax," or he would have some serious health problems in the future. The doctor suggested meditation. My friend told me that every day at the end of his lunch hour, he would put a "do not disturb" sign on his door, shut his eyes and meditate for about twenty minutes. Afterward, he felt refreshed and ready to tackle the rest of his workday. His stress related symptoms went away.

I realize not everybody can take time during the workday to meditate. So when you get home from work, take the time to unwind! I believe everybody needs to unwind after a hectic day. This book is intended to help you bring more happiness into your life. Being relaxed through the day—or, at least relaxing after a hectic day—can bring you more peace, calm, and potentially more happiness.

Chapter 10

My Morning Routine

I really don't consider myself a disciplined person in certain respects, but I *have* developed a daily morning routine. The reason I am putting it in this book is because I feel my routine puts me on the right track to start the day, and it might give you some ideas you can adapt to your life.

After I get out of bed and use the bathroom, I will go into the kitchen and make breakfast—which is usually a cup of coffee, two strips of 94% lean turkey bacon and two eggs mixed with a baked spinach quinoa cake, which I cook in coconut oil. After breakfast, I take my supplements with around a quart of water.

Next I will do Qi Gong stretching exercises, which take roughly 15 minutes. I follow that with 20 pushups, and 40 to 50 leg lifts and sit-ups.

I will then get a towel and the tub I soak my feet in, fill it up with hot water, put the tub on the towel, grab a chair and start soaking my feet. In addition, as I said in the chapter about soaking my feet, I will usually take this time to meditate as well. The meditation takes anywhere from 15 to 30 minutes.

After I am through meditating, I take a shower. I use the time in the shower as a meditation also. I focus on how good the hot water feels on my neck and shoulders, and it feels great!!

I was talking to a cousin of mine and he said he took about a 3 minute shower. I was shocked! What's the rush? If you have a busy day ahead of you, MAKE TIME to at least enjoy a long hot shower.

After the shower I make my daily "to-do" list, and out the door I go.

My routine takes roughly 2.5 hours. I admit, when I have to be somewhere at, say—8 AM, I wake up at 5 AM. I AM ready for the day!

Just like I said in Chapter 1 (If It Isn't Fun, Don't Do It!), my method probably isn't perfect for you. You are going to have to develop your own personal routine you are happy with to maximize your enjoyment.

Chapter 11

If It's Fun, Do It! (Follow Your Heart)

In Chapter 1 (If It Isn't Fun, Don't Do It!), I suggested ways to help make the unenjoyable, mundane tasks in your life more enjoyable. What about the activities we do enjoy, or activities we would like to do?

I have heard it said, "Do what you love and the money will follow." I don't know if that's true or not. What I do know, however, is when I am doing something I love, I am happy. So, I would say: "Do what you love and happiness will follow!"

I have played the guitar and mandolin for many years. When I am playing music, I feel happy! Most people I've talked to have some sort of hobby or activity they really enjoy! I have no idea what it is for you, but you do!

Before the invention of television, I believe the majority of people used their creativity much, much more than they do today. This is because they had fewer choices for filling their time, and they had to be more creative with their hands.

I believe we all have some sort of creative talent! It's just a matter of finding and nurturing it! Did you have any hobbies when you were growing up? Is there something you always wanted to learn? It could be anything you're interested in.

Maybe now is the time to figure out what your talent is! I have found that most people are naturally drawn to their talent. I can't draw to save my life! Even though my dad made me take art lessons, they did not help! Stick figures were a problem then, and still are now! I have always been good at playing musical instruments, so that is what I nurture. What are you good at?

Once you have figured it out, you are going to have to make time to do it! I have trouble with this sometimes. I know when I play music, I feel happy. I will admit it; there are times I will veg out in front of the TV. The TV is too easy an option. It's not that I don't enjoy watching TV; it's that too much time is spent in front of it at the cost of doing something else. Not to mention the violence, hate (I had mentioned earlier) and paranoia most networks subject viewers with. For the most part, I cannot find "happy" options on TV. What I suggest- instead of watching TV- is to find your creativity and nurture it!

Take out a pen and paper and make a list of all the activities you enjoy doing, all of the activities you have done in the past you enjoyed, and all of the activities you would like to do. Choose one of the activities. Start something new!

I know we live in a very fast-paced and stressful society. I believe it is important to take time to slow down, and I know it is difficult to do. Not only does the mind want to be constantly fed, but we also have everyday responsibilities. Finding your creative outlet will help with slowing down and reducing stress, because while you are spending time doing something you enjoy, you are happy.

Chapter 12

The Power of Forgiveness

I couldn't write a book on happiness if I didn't include a chapter on forgiveness. As I said in the introduction, I grew up in a very unhappy family, and I had a lot of work to do if I wanted to become happier! I didn't really start my journey toward happiness until I learned to forgive. I define forgiveness as "to stop holding resentment against something," and that something is usually a person, multiple people, or yourself.

When you have bad feelings toward someone, those feelings may or may not have any effect on that person. In fact, that person might not have any idea you are mad at him/her at all! So who does your anger hurt? It hurts you! How does holding resentment affect you? How does it make you feel? I can tell you, when I hold resentment toward someone, I feel angry, hurt, frustrated, and not totally in control.

Usually, I feel angry when a person didn't act in a way I thought or expected they should. When that happens, I hold a grudge and carry it with me everywhere I go, 24 hours a day, for the rest of my life... until I choose to let it go and forgive.

Over the years, I've had a rather tumultuous relationship with my aunt and uncle. It so happened that my brother, cousin, and I purchased a vacation property right next to theirs. Our property needed lots of work including installing water and electric service, and I was hoping (expecting) to stay with my aunt and uncle while I worked on it. I knew they had plenty of room, so I didn't think it would be a problem. But when I asked them if I could stay with them, they said "No."

Man, was I was pissed!! How could family treat family that way?

I carried that anger with me for many months, refusing to speak to them. One day, Mom mentioned to me my aunt and uncle's anniversary was coming up, and I basically said "So what?"

Shortly afterwards I started getting this feeling that I should let my resentment toward my aunt and uncle go! If only for my sake!

So I ended up slipping an anniversary card into their mailbox. The very next day, we pulled into the local library... literally, seconds apart. I got out of my truck and there they were! It's funny how life works that way sometimes. Since I had forgiven them, I was able to shake my uncle's hand and give my aunt a hug.

I can't imagine the confrontation that might have occurred had I not forgiven them and put the card in their mailbox.

When you are able to forgive, not only do you release bad feelings from your body, you allow the feelings of love to flow into yourself and out to others. In this case, it came back as a hug and a handshake. It is not always easy to forgive however...

Chapter 13

Seek Help to Forgive!

There might be times when you need assistance in forgiving someone. Personally, I have had a lot of help. As I said before, I was an unhappy person, but fortunate in that I recognized it, and open to getting help. If you are not open to getting help, it will be difficult to change.

Forgiveness doesn't have to be done face to face. One friend of mine suggests you write a letter to whomever you are holding some resentment against (dead or alive). Express everything you feel in the letter; don't hold back! Then burn the letter. If the letter burns completely, the resentment should be gone. If not, re-write the letter and give it another try. Remember, the goal is to rid you of unwanted feelings. The more unwanted feelings you get rid of, the happier you will feel.

I saw my first therapist when I was thirty-six years old. (I am now fifty-three). It's a pretty amazing story of how I met my first therapist. Life really had to throw some unexpected twists and turns my direction to allow me to experience the greatest positive change I have ever had in my life, up to this point!

My intention was to go back to college and get a teaching certificate. But that didn't exactly happen. My nephew came to visit my parents and me; he was 13 years old, and I was 36. He weighed about 100 lbs and I weighed 150. Full of energy, he wanted to wrestle with me. So we did, and I pinned him. Again and again, he jumped on me with the same results. I tired of the game, so I told him I didn't want to wrestle anymore.

I was unprepared as he jumped on me again and this time I leaned awkwardly on my right hand and broke my baby finger (the metacarpal bone to be exact). Since it was my right hand, I was unable to take notes, and missed the upcoming semester of school. I got the cast off my hand about six weeks later, with no job or school to attend. My cousin Isaac asked me to stay with him in Potomac, Maryland, where he lived—to help him with various tasks. One of these tasks was to review his accounting because I had a degree in finance.

The second night I was there, a friend of his arrived who was going to stay for a few days. Her name was Annie. She saw my guitar and asked me to play some of my original songs. After I played them to her, she said I "had some sadness in me."

I said, "I guess so."

Unbeknownst to me, she was a therapist of sorts. We debated the concept that all emotions come from either "Love" or "Fear" (her argument) until about 3 AM. I finally agreed with her. I still believe it today.

The following day, my cousin Isaac gave me his bank statements to look over to see if I had any recommendations that might help him. I looked them over and found he had $100,000 making 4% interest, and a $50,000 loan charging 8% interest... FROM THE SAME COMPANY! I was livid. I felt he was getting ripped off!

I got so angry that I could hardly speak. I had to walk around the block to cool off. Just as I started my walk, I ran into Annie and she asked me, "What's wrong?"

I angrily told her I thought Isaac was getting ripped off, and she says to me, "We need to have a session!"

Angrily, I said, "OK."

That evening, I went to her office—having no idea what to expect. She wasn't a psychiatrist—or anything I had heard of before—but I had the feeling I could trust her, so I followed her lead.

She first used kinesiology on me. This is muscle testing. The basic theory behind kinesiology is that your body has intelligence separate from your mind. You can ask yes or no questions, or make statements like... "My name is Mary." Since my name isn't Mary, my muscles will go weak. When I tell the truth, my muscles remain strong.

This was all new to me! But, as I said earlier, I felt like I could trust Annie... so I just went with it. Through the kinesiology, Annie somehow determined I had (as she put it) some energy blocks against my Mom. I didn't understand what she meant by "energy blocks," plus I totally disagreed with her! Mom and I were very close and really got along well. Again, I felt like I could trust Annie, so I went along with the program. Her explanation of the energy blocks had to do with how energy naturally flows through our body according to Chinese medicine and acupuncture.

Next she had me lay down on a couch and played a tape of dolphin song. She said the song of the dolphin helps us remember past memories. Again, as strange as I thought it was, I went with it... She asked me to remember the earliest bad memory I had with my mom. At the same time, she asked me to start deep breathing, she had me tap on my thymus gland, and with my other hand, place my thumb and index finger about 4 inches apart on my forehead.

The first memory that came to me had to do with my sister Pam and I having to give toys to Goodwill, because each year we received so many. Pam and I were a year and a day apart in age, and we basically got the same toys. I would usually tear mine up a bit, whereas Pam's were like brand new. One time, we were each given this clown thing (all I can remember about it), and I kept mine in better shape than Pam did. I was very proud of this!

The next thing I remember is the Goodwill man carrying a bag of toys out of our front door, with my clown thing on top of it. I remember pointing at it and screaming.

"WAAA!!! WAAA!!!" I can't remember how old I was, but I was young enough that Mom was able to pick me up, and she asked me, "What's the matter... What's the matter?"

She was not able to understand what I wanted, and my clown thing was gone... out of my life forever!

As I tell Annie this story, tears start flowing... big time! I couldn't believe my mom gave my clown thing away! I am tapping and breathing the entire time.

Annie asks me, "Do you think your mom would have given your clown thing away if she knew how much it had meant to you?"

"Well... no," I answered (Still tapping and breathing).

"Do you think you can forgive her for giving away your clown thing?"

"Well, yes I can."

"Say it!" Annie says.

So I say it. "I forgive you, Mom... for giving away my clown thing."

The evening continued as I recalled a few alcoholic memories with my mom (me still tapping and breathing). Annie pointed out that alcoholism is a disease and asked me if I could forgive someone who is sick? I said "of course" I could, and forgave mom for that...

The session ended, and Annie asked how I felt. I told her I felt a bit light headed. She gave me some orange juice, I sat for a while, and then she sent me on my way.

The next morning- at breakfast- I told Isaac I thought he should sell enough stock to pay off the loan, and I explained the details. He really didn't say much at the time. At 10 AM, his secretary was due in, and we were going to have a meeting. After she arrived, Isaac (using a very condescending voice) says, "I'm taking Larry off the finances—he just doesn't have enough experience!"

Not only was I shocked at what Isaac said, but I was really surprised at my reaction! My brain was saying, "You son of a ..." but my gut was saying, "We have *no* problems down here!"

I looked at Isaac, and said "I'd have killed you yesterday." I wouldn't have killed him, but I probably would have left the room in a fury, being so upset and hurt. Then, I laughed! And I knew I had changed. My wicked temper was gone, and much, much more.

One thing that amazes me about this experience is how a seemingly innocent act—like getting rid of a toy—might have such a profound effect on a child. I know that it affected me until I forgave mom and let the resentment go. Looking back at it, my mom probably gave my clown thing away because she didn't understand the significance I tied to it. Maybe, this was in part because of its' pristine condition.

To this day, I don't remember what Annie's title was, but her therapy combined forgiveness coaching along with body energy work. Body energy work helps remove blocked energy stored in your body due to unresolved mental issues.

I'm sure all of you have heard the expression "You pushed my buttons."

In my opinion, buttons are blocked energy. We all seem to have "buttons" that will trigger strong, uncontrollable emotional or physical responses. I have found when you are able to clear the particular energy block (button) from your body, you will no longer be subject to its effect or your uncontrollable reaction. As a result, you will feel lighter and happier. I know I do!

Words cannot express the love and gratitude I have for Annie. She helped me and expected nothing in return. Her kindness was certainly an act of unconditional love... something unusual to receive from somebody I hardly knew. Not only did she help me free myself from some of my past hurts and resentments, but she also gifted me with a method that would allow me to become happier, and help others, as well.

With great sadness, I must tell you that Annie Bhasin has passed away after a bout with cancer. However, I see two women who do similar work here in Cincinnati: Anne Steffen, and Blu Fries. I will call this work "Forgiveness Therapy," and provide their contact information in the back of the book.

The great news is: this type of therapy is done all over the country and throughout the world! I believe it is far superior to traditional types of therapy because it removes the energy behind the emotional issues.

There is an amazing book that I highly recommend; a book written by Louise Hay, called "You Can Heal Your Life." The basic premise of her book is that we create 'dis-ease' with our thinking. So, in turn, we can heal ourselves with our thinking.

At the end the book, she lists various diseases and ailments that we can suffer from. She lists the ailment, the probable cause, and the new thought pattern to heal the ailment. For example, Ms. Hay states that if you have anxiety, the probable cause is "not trusting the flow of life." The new thought pattern is "I love and approve of myself and I trust the process of life. I am safe." I believe this goes hand in hand with the "forgiveness therapy" I mentioned before. They both are getting rid of old thought patterns (buttons... blocked energy). The other day my knee swelled up, so I called Blu, in this instance. She determined and helped me resolve an issue with my brother. My knee was much better afterward.

Another book I have to mention is "The Four Agreements: A Practical Guide to Personal Freedom, A Toltec Wisdom Book" written by Don Miguel Ruiz. This is a must read! He explains that thousands of years ago, the Toltec—who were an ancient civilization—attempted to tackle the subject of how to become happy (I am paraphrasing).

Basically, every human's mind is invaded by a parasite. He compares the parasite to a monster with 1000 heads. When we get rid of the parasite, we will be happy.

The "forgiveness" therapy in my opinion is a way to get rid of the heads of the parasite, blocked energy, old thought patterns or buttons. There are many names for the same condition. Again, I highly recommend reading "The Four Agreements."

I can't explain how the "forgiveness" therapy works! I am only experiencing it! Trust me; I am totally amazed at the results!

I believe our thoughts and beliefs can, and do create stress, which also creates dis-ease within our body. When you can forgive and release the energy blocks, old thought patterns (buttons), or resentments you hold close—I believe you will be happier and healthier.

DON'T BE AFRAID TO LIE ON THE PROVERBIAL COUCH! Annie started me on the road to forgiving both my parents and a lot of anger toward myself!

You see, I had a lot of anger and frustration toward myself because I could never please my parents, resulting in me becoming a perfectionist. Being a perfectionist is quite difficult.

"Nobody is perfect," especially me! No matter how hard I tried, I was never happy with myself or happy in general. Since releasing much of the anger I felt toward my parents, and some of the anger toward myself, I have been on this amazing road toward feeling happier. I will admit, occasionally I still try to be perfect...

Chapter 14

Being a Perfectionist

I believe myself to be a recovering perfectionist. What is a perfectionist?

According to Webster's pocket dictionary, a perfectionist is: One who strives to be perfect.

What is it to be perfect? According to Webster's:

1. Complete.
2. Excellent.
3. Completely accurate.

Let's go with completely accurate. I want to add a little to that: completely accurate *all the time*. Quite frankly, I was afraid to make any mistake because of the lack of patience I received from my parents growing up (my perception of things).

Now, I don't want to mislead you. I was never that over-achiever who got straight A's, or anything like that. My perfectionist tendencies would manifest if I made any mistake, resulting in me quickly getting angry and calling myself names (as I mentioned earlier in the book). As I continue my work on happiness using the "forgiveness therapy," I have become more patient with myself. I now consider myself—more often than not—a person who "works on doing the best job they can" in any given situation, as opposed to being a perfectionist.

What is the difference between being a perfectionist and doing the best job you can? I believe it has to do with how angry you get if/when you make a mistake. I believe when you are a perfectionist you will obsess and get angry if the task that is being performed isn't "perfect." Where doing the best job you can, will end with the same result... without the anger or obsessive behavior.

Some of the traits I am talking about are: getting mad at yourself and/or others, short bursts of anger, and feelings of frustration- just to name a few- if the task you are engaged in isn't being done "perfectly."

I believe it is important for YOU to start recognizing the perfectionist traits within yourself, because they are an indication there are energy blocks that can be cleared. Once you start clearing your energy blocks, you can start being "somebody who works at doing the best job they can."

The immediate thing you can do once you've recognized a perfectionistic trait rising, is to stop and take a deep breath… after the situation is past, I call Blu Fries or Anne Steffen and set up an appointment to start helping me work on clearing up this "button" that was pushed—which caused my perfectionist behavior to raise its ugly head.

I also believe the "need to be right" is another perfectionist trait…

Chapter 15

Being Right Is Over-Rated!

I believe the "need to be right" is a perfectionistic trait. What do I mean by "being right?" It is an overwhelming desire to feel victorious no matter how insignificant the subject is. This results in having petty arguments just to prove another person wrong, and to be able to say you're right, and "I told you so!" When you are right, you are perfect. All this, I believe, is related to self-worth and self-love (see Chapter 27).

A couple of friends of mine got married; educated, successful, attractive, seemingly happy people. I really didn't know them well, but when I was around them, I noticed they were always bickering with each other. The times I heard the bickering, it was about stupid little things that didn't matter, but was important for one of them to be right! They ended up getting a divorce!

I was with a friend of mine and we were listening to NPR. A story came on about somebody who won a trip to Antarctica. I half-jokingly, half seriously made the comment of "Oh boy! What a prize!" What I expected my friend to do was either to laugh at my comment, or agree. Never having heard my friend say he had any desire to go to Antarctica, and never, ever meeting anybody who wanted to go to Antarctica, I was quite shocked when he rebutted my statement. At that moment I was wrong and he was right. I could have debated with him, but what was the point?

There is no winner when the game of "Being Right" is played. You might get a boost for your ego, but if you are "right," then somebody else is "wrong" and bad feelings are created.

Of course, making the right choice or decision is important... but "being right" for its own sake is a detriment.

As I stated earlier in this chapter, I expected my friend to act a certain way. What I have found is, the less you expect, the happier you will be!

Chapter 16

Unrealistic Expectations

How many times have you been in a situation where you expected a certain thing to happen—but it didn't—and you were disappointed? It could be the big party your friend had; though it was fun, it just wasn't as much fun as you expected it to be, and you were disappointed. You expected a promotion at work, but got passed over for somebody else—and even though you liked the job you had, it was never quite as enjoyable afterward. Or, like in the drawing, you expect to get the hamburger you saw in the commercial, but you get a smaller, less impressive one…

It seems to me the ONLY time we can be disappointed is when we expect something and don't get it. Without expectations, you won't be disappointed. Having expectations is an attempt to predict the future. I don't know about you, but I'm not very good at it, especially when talking about behaviors or feelings. Is it possible to go through life without expectations?

In my opinion, attempting to go through life without expectations is nearly impossible. This is because we all have base line expectations of our family, our friends, ourselves, and life in general. These I believe are natural, but having them can still cause disappointment.

I believe if we work toward eliminating *unrealistic* expectations, or being too critical or too judgmental toward ourselves and others, we will all be happier, and will be able to establish a base level of contentment…

Chapter 17

Contentment and Gratitude

Having a base level of contentment with our current situation is really the only way to be happy in the current moment. Since the current moment is the only moment we ever have, if we aren't happy NOW, when are we going to be?

I had a friend who was never happy. She was always wishing for things in the future to "make" her happy. "I wish I had a boyfriend..." She got a boyfriend. "I wish I had a different boyfriend... I wish I had this, I wish I had that." It didn't matter what she had, she was never happy in the moment. She was always striving for that "thing" that would make her happy in the future.

When I say, "be content with what you have," I don't mean stop striving to improve your situation. I mean stop and be grateful for what you do have. You never know, this could be as good as it gets!

During the past recession I pretty much invested all of my money in real estate. It wasn't that I did anything anybody would consider risky at all. It was just really bad timing. I wanted to start a new career and I figured real estate would be a safe bet, because everybody needs a place to live. So I bought 2 houses, one I lived in, and another was a rental. I fixed them up and put them on the market to sell.

After 4 years of paying $3300 per month carrying these properties waiting for them to sell, I ran out of money. Boy, was I grateful to have friends hire me to do various odd jobs!

The property I lived in was on 3.6 acres, and had a stream in the back where previous owners over the years would dump "stuff." One day while I was walking around the property, I noticed some metal sticking out of the stream. It was a piece of aluminum. I then discovered there was a good amount of loose metal all over my property, so I started to scrap it.

Any money I had was what I earned day to day, and it wasn't much. At one point during this time period—the worst of which lasted around 2 years—I must have had a decent day scrapping, or painting. In any case, I figured out that I had enough money to buy 100 days of food—just in case. This is where my head was at.

Anyhow, during this time I was forced to eat beans and cheese 4 to 5 days a week. Eventually, I learned to love and appreciate having beans and cheese for a meal... add a little spice; they are pretty tasty and filling!

I learned many things during this very scary time period in my life. One was that having the basics of food, shelter, and clothing is truly something to be grateful for! There are people all over the world who are struggling to meet their basic needs, and many live in war zones. Another thing I learned was to be content with what I had. I was warm and dry and fed! Just look around! We all have so much to be grateful for!

At this point, I highly suggest you make a "GRATITUDE LIST."

Go and get a piece of paper and write down all of the things you are truly grateful for! Take your time with this. Put the list in a place where you can easily get to it. Whenever you are feeling troubled about something, get out your list and read it over and over again. It will help you refocus by taking your mind off of what is troubling you, and help you realize you indeed are truly fortunate.

Choose to feel gratitude for what you do have, and don't be unhappy for what you don't have. In most cases, you don't NEED what you don't have.

What I am going to tell you next might have been the most important lesson I learned during this time, which was learning to live in the moment...

Chapter 18

Living in the Moment

I was forced to live in the moment! I had foreclosures hanging over my head, the possibility of me losing my home and being thrown out on the street, harassing phone calls from creditors, and no steady income. If I thought about all of the above, it paralyzed me with fear. There was one particular time when I was curled up in a ball, whimpering like a dog feeling sorry for myself, when I realized; "in this moment" I am truly alright! I am warm, I am dry, and I am fed!

"Living in the moment" pulls many topics in this book together. I used to constantly dwell on the past and worry about the future. The past is something nobody needs to think about because it's done and gone, unless you're looking at it to learn or forgive. Worrying about the future is a game of speculation, and while you are worrying about it, you are hurting your present moment. Anytime you focus on the past or the future, you miss out on the present moment. What I have found is most of my present moments are pretty darn good! I'm not starving; I'm not in pain; I'm not too hot or cold; I'm breathing fresh air; I have a roof over my head; a bed to sleep in at night...I think you get the idea! Life is good in the present moment. Problems arise when we leave the present moment and start worrying about the "what-ifs" in life. Even if the "what-ifs'" do happen in the future, they are not happening now!

I went to the dentist the other day to get a tooth crowned. Even though I am treating myself like royalty, I don't like getting a crown! I admit, for the time I was in the dentist chair, I wanted to be anywhere but "in the moment!" LOL! I was grateful however, that I was able to get my teeth worked on.

To sum it up: As you are treating yourselves like the Kings and Queens you truly are, when you get into your comfortable bed (be in the moment)! When you take your comfortable shower (be in the moment)! When you put on your comfy robe and slippers (be in the moment)! When you soak your feet (be in the moment)! When you meditate (be in the moment)!

One amazing thing I realized when I was in the worst of times, was I still had everything I needed to treat myself like royalty, in the moment.

The more you are in the moment, the happier you will be. One of the easiest places to be in the moment is when you are in nature...

Chapter 19

Spend Time in Nature

Spending time in nature is an amazing way to bring more happiness into your life. Why do I say this? One reason is that nature expects nothing of you. No worries in nature. In a sense, nature is solely there for you to enjoy! It's no coincidence I placed this chapter directly after "Living in the Moment." Nature, in my opinion, is a gift and a demonstration of living in the moment. Being in nature is a total "in the moment" experience. Watch the birds fly; listen to the birds sing; hear the sound of leaves crunch beneath your feet; breathe in the fresh air. "Oh look! A squirrel just ran by!" If you can shut everything in your mind out, except what is going on around you, you will find yourself starting to slow down and relax. If you can, take a walk every day!

While I was in college, my friend Craig wanted to go camping at Red River Gorge at Daniel Boone National Park in Kentucky. We left at around 7 that evening, and arrived at the park around 10 o'clock that night. We put our backpacks on and started to hike using flashlights to be able to see. After an hour or so I began to complain about "all" the studying and homework I had to do. Craig turns to me and says, "We are an hour hike away from the car and 180 miles from Cincinnati. The only things you need to worry about up here are where you are going to spend the night, and your next step…" I realized he was absolutely right. So I quit my complaining and enjoyed the camping trip.

I feel happier when I am in nature than when I am anywhere else. I feel calmer, more relaxed, and more connected to God/ Source/ the Creator of all things!

Chapter 20

Spirituality

I am a very spiritual man. I feel it is important to include what I personally believe, because what I believe is the foundation of my happiness. I want to assure all of you that my beliefs are mine, and yours are yours. I am not trying to convince you to change your beliefs in anyway. What I hope you will do is to look at your beliefs and make sure they SERVE YOU, and make YOU happy!

It won't do you much good if you "think" you believe in something because that is how you were raised, and you are following your parents' beliefs. At the end of the day, yours are the only beliefs that should matter to you! Search your heart for the answers. Then, take a look at your beliefs and change what doesn't make you happy. What I am talking about are your feelings.

What I have learned is my beliefs aren't any better or any worse than anybody else's, and they don't make me any better or any worse than anybody else.

I will say this, however- if your beliefs have anything to do with harming or forcing your will upon another person, you are not in touch with your heart, you are listening to your ego!

I wasn't raised with any formal religion to speak of. I was raised a Unitarian. What my parents told me was that I could believe in whatever I wanted to believe.

Both of my parents, their parents, and their ancestors all the way back were Jewish. Dad was raised Orthodox, Mom a reformed Jew.

When Dad was young, one of his sisters died at an early age and he became disillusioned with God. Even though they were married by a Rabbi, at some point they became Unitarians. This particular Unitarian church in my opinion was more of a social club. I can't remember being taught anything about religion, however as long as I can remember, I FELT there was something greater than myself! There are many names the various religions call the creator of all things, I will use "God/Source."

I'll be the first one to admit that I have no idea what God/Source is, or what God/Source's plan is... I just believe there is a God/Source of some sort, and he/she/they have a plan. The important thing is I feel good believing this! I have faith!

I am going to tell you various possibilities I have read about spiritual matters that make sense, and feel right to me. They give me confidence, hope and comfort. This is what I want for you!

First of all, I believe in intelligent design. Just look around you at all the complex ecological systems in nature, for starters. I also believe in evolution. I believe life was designed to evolve to a point. I don't believe it was just random luck over billions of years that created the various life forms. For example: Look at this diagram of the bones in the inner ear of a human being. These 3 oddly shaped bones have to fit exactly in the ear for us to hear.

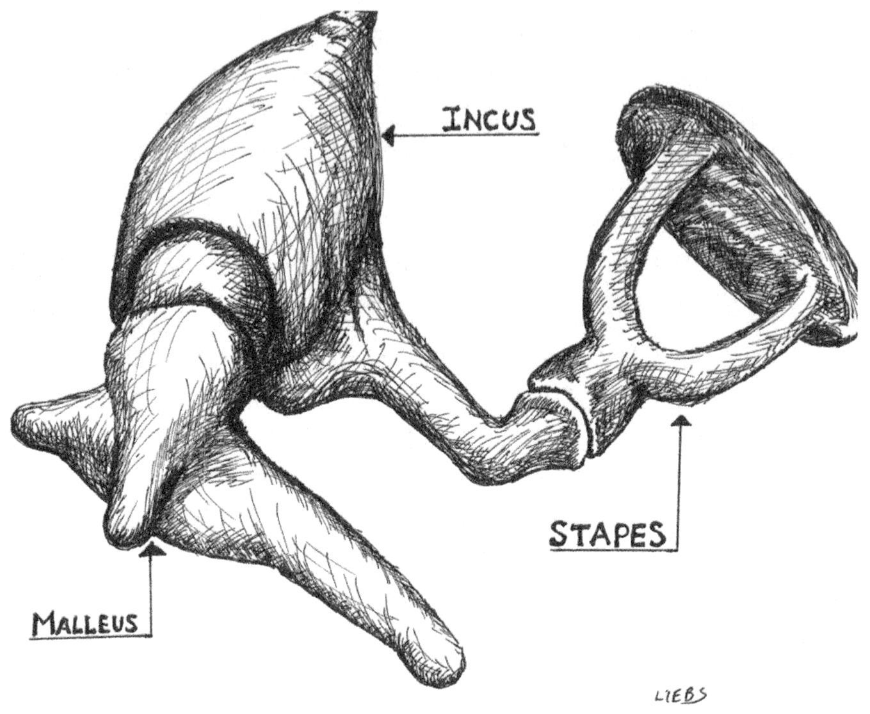

I believe it was designed.

How does the idea of intelligent design feel to you?

I believe we have a soul/spirit and we live many, many life times, to learn and develop our soul.

I have read many books that talk about people who have remembered past lives. One of my favorites is "Many Lives, Many Masters" written by Dr. Brian Weiss. Dr. Weiss is a medically and scientifically trained Psychiatrist. While helping a client, after he put her under hypnosis, she started speaking ancient languages she couldn't possibly know.

I don't believe there is any reason for Dr. Weiss to be untruthful in what he witnessed while working on his client. Being a prominent member in his field, he put his reputation on the line by writing his book. In his book, as he reports it, he is stunned and amazed at what he observed.

When I finished reading "Many Lives, Many Masters," I was afraid to go to sleep because I realized that anything is possible! It shook me! But it also felt right.

Something to consider is the child prodigy. For example: Look at Mozart. Why and how was he born with the musical ability of an adult and then some? Another benefit for me in believing in more than one lifetime, is when a loved one dies...you will see them again. It doesn't stop the pain of missing them in this lifetime, but it helps. Einstein said that energy is never lost, it just takes another form.

"Many Lives, Many Masters" was my first introduction to the possibility of us having a soul/spirit. I now believe it. As I stated before, I believe we live many, many life times to learn and grow, and everything we experience is a lesson for our soul. I will admit, I don't know exactly what the lessons are. My hunch is love, compassion, and patience toward others and ourselves. We could all use more of these lessons. I believe love, compassion and patience toward ourselves is a major step to finding happiness!

How does the idea of having past lives feel to you?

In addition, I believe we are all simultaneously teacher and students. I don't care how old somebody is, if they're male, female, their income level, religion, or occupation... if I am open to it, if I am listening, I might be able to learn from them. This is because they are experiencing life from their own unique perspective and they might have some insight I don't. Plus, you never know- they might be an old soul.

How does the idea of us all being simultaneously students and teachers feel to you?

I believe if we can be quiet enough, we can be guided by our intuition. One problem I personally have, is what I will call monkey mind. Some people call it mind chatter. I think so much, I have a hard time discerning what is intuition, versus what are random thoughts. The major problem in our modern day society, I believe, is there are too many distractions to keep us from seeing, hearing or feeling the guidance. I believe the more you follow your intuition, the happier you will be.

How does the idea of being guided by our intuition feel to you?

Chapter 21

Free Will vs. Predestination

I have been searching for a definitive answer to this question my entire life! I am still not convinced one way or another. The answer seems to be a combination of both.

There have been a few times where I dreamt a future event that occurred. One was the score of the Cincinnati Reds game the following day. I was pretty amazed when, near the end of the game, a player hit a home run to make the score as I had dreamt it. The other time I was looking for a job. I dreamt that I went to a former General Manager of a hotel I had worked for, filled out an application and he gave me a job. After I woke up, I went to the hotel the General Manager was working at, filled out the application and he gave me a job.

Does this mean that everything is already planned out? Do we have a defined life path? If so, where does free will come into play? A conversation I had with a friend summed it up pretty well for me. We do have free will, but only under a limited set of choices. Does this also mean we have more than one life path we can follow, but there is a limited number?

It seems to me, moment to moment, we can make yes or no decisions. I will do this, I won't do that… I will have a salad, not a hamburger… but what/or who determined that I am allergic to certain foods? So… I won't have the hamburger. I'd better have the salad, but no red onions or tomatoes.

So let's say we have free will choices moment to moment. What is less clear to me, however, is whether we can control the outcome of our choices and actions. Sure, the simple ones… "I will get out of the chair… I will turn to the left or to the right…"

What about the BIG choices? For example, I am writing this book. I can get it published. But I can't control if anybody will read it, or if anybody will enjoy it for that matter. Why haven't I won the lottery yet? I've played it long enough! Maybe I'm not supposed to, because it will interfere with a spiritual lesson tied to money (see Chapter 23). I keep playing, though! What do you think?

How do you feel about free will versus predestination?

If we don't control the outcome of our actions, then who or what does control these things?

Chapter 22

Control

"Let go and let God." I'm sure most of you have heard this saying. This is where my belief system really kicks in. When things go well, I thank God/Source. When things go bad, I do my best to find the lesson I am supposed to learn and figure God/Source has a reason for me to experience "whatever." If something doesn't work out the way I had planned, I just figure it wasn't meant to be!

Now, I'm not saying if something I interpret as being bad happens to me, or if my world is turned upside down and I have to eat beans and cheese 4 to 5 times a week, that I am happy about it (I'm not there yet). I am saying it is important for EACH of us to develop a belief system that helps us "roll" with the punches and make it through the hard times.

As unstable as our world affairs are, I believe it is part of a master plan of God/source. I have no idea what that plan is! One reason I believe this is because- in my opinion- as chaotic as our world is, it has to be planned! I don't believe our world could be this chaotic accidentally!

The world would run smoothly if humans were not here. Do you think Mother Nature created humans just to mess up the eco system? In any case, if the fate of the world is left up to us humans alone- in my opinion- we are doomed!

Fortunately, I believe in a power greater than myself, and I am happy to give up my illusion of control to it! I believe one way God/Source exerts its control is through spiritual lessons.

How do you feel about giving up control to God/Source?

Chapter 23

Spiritual Lessons

Have you ever been in a situation where you were between a rock and a hard place? A situation where whatever choice you had to make would not turn out well for you? Or everything you had planned didn't work out? At times like these, I believe it's a spiritual lesson.

I was in a situation where one friend explained a predicament they were in with another friend of mine. After they told me what they were planning to do, they asked me what I thought.

First of all, I disagreed with my friend's proposal. My problem was, if I said nothing or did nothing, I knew my other friend would be hurt, and I couldn't live with myself. If I agreed with the friend who asked me my opinion, I knew my other friend would be hurt. If I told my friend I disagreed with them, then they would be mad at me. So what do I do? I am screwed either way!

I ended up telling my friend I disagreed with them, and they were mad at me. We did not speak for many, many months.

So let me sum it up. I was given information I did not ask for, and it put me in a no-win situation. I had to make a choice- which I did, and it hurt me.

As I reviewed my situation after many months went by, I realized it had to be a spiritual lesson of some sort. And what do I mean by spiritual lesson? It is a situation that is placed in your path by God/source to help you learn and grow.

I believe whenever anybody is in a no win-situation not of their making, it has to be spiritual. Once I accepted the situation as spiritual, I was able to forgive myself, and my friend. We still were not speaking at the time, but I "let go and let God". Shortly afterward, a mutual friend got us to sit down together and talk things out. We made up and are still very close to this day.

I believe I was put into this situation for a reason, along with many other situations in my life I had no control over... as we all are. I believe this happens to teach us, but to teach us *what*? Sometimes you can figure it out, other times; who knows? The experiences I had during my financial crisis I believe were spiritual lessons. The most important one I believe was to learn to live in the moment. Whenever I experience a spiritual lesson, I just have faith it's for my own good, and is leading me on the path to being happier.

How do you feel about "Spiritual Lessons?"

Many times like these I feel the need to surrender.

Chapter 24

Surrender

I believe we all have an idea of what it means to surrender. Basically it's to give one's self up. The idea I would like to get across is to surrender to the way things are, and putting it in God/Sources hands (if there is nothing you can do about it). Hopefully, the following example will help clarify.

During my financial crisis, I had a mortgage on a piece of property that was an old farm. I love the farm! I can see myself retiring there someday. There are 72 acres, a stocked pond, and an amazing view where you can yell… and it will echo back! I have had many a camp out, building large fires and playing music with several friends.

I did everything thing I could to keep it from going into foreclosure. I'd send the bank $100 here, $100 there, to try to buy time. For a while, the bank was willing to work with me. Then, one day the foreclosure process began, and at the time there was nothing I could do about it. I was crushed! What a beautiful property! What a shame it would be if I lost the farm.

One afternoon, I was visiting my neighbors Jeff and Marlene, and we were sitting outside in their back yard. They take great pride in how their yard looks! The sun was shining; I was looking around at all of the beautiful flowers they had planted and the meandering stream that flowed through their property. Then it occurred to me! There are beautiful places and beauty everywhere! In addition, *I* bring the beauty, depending upon how I interpret what I am looking at.

At that moment, I realized if I lost the farm, it would be OK… I could find another beautiful place. I surrendered to the certainty of losing the farm, and I was at peace with it. If God/source wanted me to keep the farm, great! If not, it wasn't meant to be.

The very next week, events fell into place where I was able to keep the farm—an amazing story in itself, but one for another day.

How do you feel about surrendering a situation to God/Source?

Chapter 25

The Big Bang Theory

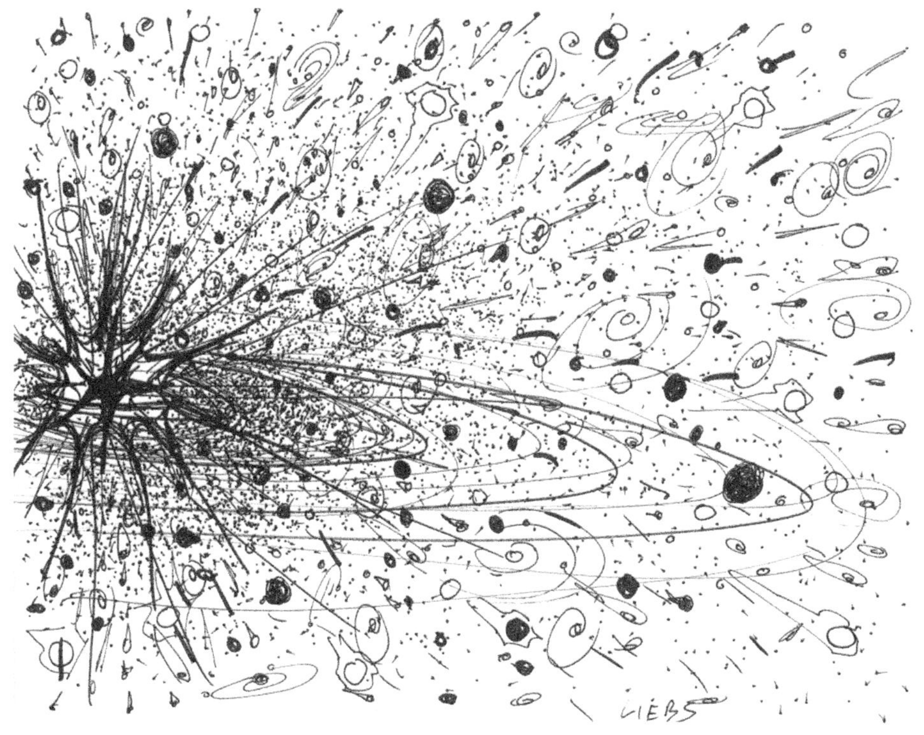

I believe most people have an idea what the "Big Bang Theory" is (and not the TV show). But for those who don't know, I will give you a brief summation.

Basically, the theory is that our universe was an extremely dense ball of matter, which for some unknown reason suddenly exploded outward into billions of pieces, and is still expanding to this day.

So why am I telling you all about the "Big Bang Theory"? Because, it shows me we are all part of the whole. We are all related to everything, and to each other. I have read or heard one explanation of the age-old question of "Why are we here?" The answer being; we are all pieces of God/Source, learning and expressing. I like this!

If the "Big Bang Theory" is true, then people are more alike than different. So why in our world do we focus on the differences in people as opposed to the similarities? Let me suggest the next time you see somebody different from you, to remember we all come from the same origin.

Again, I put this into the book for you to consider how you FEEL about it.

Chapter 26

The Perception of Love

What I am finding as I continue doing the "forgiveness therapy" and contemplating what happiness is, at the end of the day, I want to feel loved all the time, and I believe everybody else does, too. What makes this interesting and also complicated, is there are many different ways to express and receive love. What feels like love to one person might not feel like love to another.

I believe what we learn in our childhood about love greatly determines our "style of behavior," and how we perceive we are feeling loved, and in turn how we give love.

For example: I had a few dates with a woman who didn't like her parents. She told me her mother, in particular, wasn't very enjoyable to be around. However, her mother's one saving grace was she would give extravagant gifts. On our third date, she told me why she didn't want to date me; one of her reasons was because she wanted nice things, and didn't believe I could give them to her.

I was taken aback by this, thinking she was only after money. That was our last date. As I reviewed the dates in my mind (I really liked this woman), I remembered what she had said about her mother's only saving grace. It occurred to me her way of feeling loved was to "get nice things," because that is how her mother showed her love.

Since we determine our happiness by how we interpret life, I believe it is important for all of us to be aware of what makes us feel loved, and what upsets us. We can then have more compassion and understanding with ourselves, and communicate our needs with our significant other for them to gain understanding.

A friend of mine told me he was out with his girlfriend watching a sporting event on TV. He was happily watching the event, drinking beer as his girlfriend was getting madder and madder. He had no idea why she was getting so upset but knew she was mad at HIM!

So he asks her, "Are we fighting?" It ended up that she was shocked and unhappy with how many beers he was drinking. I believe understanding and communication would have greatly helped this situation.

I believe the most important aspect of the perception of love is how we perceive ourselves.

Chapter 27

Self-Love

I would say the underlying theme of this book is to put you in the frame of mind to love yourself. I believe once you feel love toward yourself, you will have put into place a solid foundation on which the feeling of happiness is the perspective you interpret life from.

Who would you say is your greatest critic? You, right? You spend the most time with yourself, don't you? You know every mistake you've made, don't you? Who gives you the most grief or praise? It's you!

Certainly, there are lots of people who are extremely critical and judgmental. I ought to know... I am a recovering perfectionist! The words that come out of their mouths say more about them than about you. If somebody yells and screams at you, what does that say about you? Nothing! If you are doing the yelling and screaming, what does that say about you? Everything!

The love you seek is inside yourself. You cannot find love outside of yourself because you interpret everything! You might buy something you think "made" you happy. But in reality, *you made yourself* happy because you bought something. As I said earlier in the book, how you interpret life in a given moment will determine how happy you are in that moment.

I believe when you reach the point of loving yourself, you will have the greatest possibility of being happy in each moment.

Chapter 28

Pass the "Attitude of Happiness" On to Your Children

Assuming you are going to adopt some of the suggestions in this book, I encourage you to pass them onto your children. I don't mean spoil your children. What I mean is they are part of your Royal family! My parents seemed to have an attitude that my siblings and I were "second-class citizens." While they had new beds, a working air conditioner, and a brand new TV, we had hand-me-downs. Some of the hand-me-downs were OK, others were not. It wasn't like they couldn't afford to treat us the way they treated themselves, they just didn't.

Just because you're a child, doesn't mean you don't deserve to be treated like Royalty! Along the lines that we could have lived many past lives, we will never know how wise children are, unless we listen to them with an open mind. Most likely as they get older, they will be better than us at some things. That's OK and it's perfectly natural. We all have our strengths and weaknesses. My oldest brother told me the first time he beat my Dad in a game of chess, my dad never played him again...

If you are treated like a second-class citizen, you start believing you *are* a second-class citizen. Treat your children the way you wish to be treated! This can foster happiness across many generations.

Chapter 29

Conclusion

The information you have read in this book is a compilation of ideas, practices and beliefs I have learned and accepted over the years that have helped me become happier. Most of them I figured out on my own, some I read about, and others I had help with.

I didn't start out thinking if I did "this, that, or the other thing," I would bring happiness into my life. I just started out trying to make life a little easier, less stressful, and more comfortable. The by-product I found was indeed, I was happier, feeling better about myself, and life in general! In addition, I realized I was the only one who could control my own happiness (feelings) by the way I viewed life. Nobody can "make" me mad. When I interpret a particular situation in a negative way, I make *myself* mad. The instant you blame somebody else for how you feel, you are giving away your power! You must take responsibility for your own feelings!

This book shows you how to bring more happiness into your life by attitude, comfort, belief systems, purchasing, exercise, meditation, organization, forgiveness, and self-love. I really believe self-love is the key to develop a solid foundation of happiness.

So much of this book is about self-love. Treat yourself like royalty is self-love, Purchasing to foster happiness is self-love, honoring our self with house hold items is self-love, and diet and exercise are self-love, just to mention a few. I believe anything you do (regardless of how simple it is) with the intention of bringing joy, and/or self-improvement to yourself, is an act of self-love.

As I stated earlier, I believe the "forgiveness therapy" is a method to becoming happier. Every time I forgive someone-including myself, I feel calmer, lighter, and happier.

Your viewpoint, from which you interpret your life, changes. Your outlook changes too, because you have released feelings that caused you grief. It's almost like you are submerged in water and held down by hateful feelings. Each time you release one of these hateful feelings, you start rising toward the surface, toward a fuller, happier life.

I am truly excited for all of you who decide to embark on the journey of happiness! It's a worthwhile journey I enjoy every day!

Reading this book, along with the others I suggested, is a good start! Don't be afraid or too stubborn to seek help! The individuals who choose to help people as a profession, like Anne and Blu, are very kind and caring! There is absolutely nothing to worry about!

My main reason for writing this book is to live in a happier world, by helping people become happier. This book could be part of my autobiography. You know a lot about me. I didn't hold much back... but knowing me isn't what's important!

What's important is for YOU to know YOU! Learn to love yourself, become happier and spread it to other people! Only YOU have the power to do this!

When more and more people become happier, the happiness that flows from them will ripple out into the world and change it for the better! I truly believe in this "Ripple Effect of Happiness." It starts with YOU!

HAVE A GREAT DAY!!!

Acknowledgements

I'd like to give thanks to Annie and Paul Bhasin; Annie who truly accelerated my journey toward finding happiness, and her husband Paul who allowed her to help strangers like me, by supporting her work. To Allison Head, who helped me with one round of editing. To Joe Riddle and Julie Russell, who allowed me to work at their house, feed me, and allowed Mark the use of their computer. To Dave and Deb Rudolph, for their kindness, generosity, their ability to create many happy moments, and their spark of inspiration to start this book. To Blu Fries, who helped motivate me by letting me write with her at her beautiful place along the river- not to mention, she did the second round of editing. In addition, she and Ann Steffen- who are both very talented, intuitive health care practitioners- have helped me reach a point in my life where I feel happy enough to write a book on happiness. Also, to Ann Weber who put the book in the proper form to give to the publisher. To Marlene Ceo Grimmeissen who came up with the title of the book. Last, but not least, to Mark Lieberman who did all the illustrations, the cover, and the computer aspects of getting this book ready with a handshake agreement.

I am very grateful to have these people in my life and as my friends!

Contact Information

About the Illustrator

The illustrations in this book, while not erudite, are deliberately simple and approachable. This treatment best compliments the author's sensible, down-to-earth message regarding happiness in today's world.

Mark Lieberman is an artist and craftsman who dabbles in painting, sculpting, woodworking and cooking. He lives in Cincinnati with his dog, Vinny. Reach him at: liebermonster5@gmail.com

Made in the USA
Las Vegas, NV
29 November 2021